Congressional
Research Service
Informing the legislative debate since 1914

Health Insurance Exchanges: Health Insurance "Navigators" and In-Person Assistance

Suzanne M. Kirchhoff
Analyst in Health Care Financing

August 13, 2014

Congressional Research Service

7-5700

www.crs.gov

R43243

Summary

The 2010 Patient Protection and Affordable Care Act (ACA, P.L. 111-148) allows certain individuals and small businesses to buy qualified health insurance through state exchanges. The exchanges are not themselves insurers, but rather are special marketplaces where insurance firms may sell health policies that meet set, federal guidelines. As of July 2014, 14 states and the District of Columbia had secured HHS approval to create and run their own exchanges, 7 to enter into partnership exchanges, 29 to have federally facilitated exchanges, and two to have state-based SHOP/federally facilitated individual exchanges. An estimated 25 million individuals are expected to secure coverage through the exchanges by 2024.

The ACA requires exchanges to perform outreach to help consumers and small businesses make informed decisions about their insurance options, including the operation of "navigator" programs. Navigators carry out public education activities; provide information to prospective enrollees about insurance options and federal assistance; and examine enrollees' eligibility for other federal or state health care programs, such as Medicaid. Navigators may assist consumers in comparing insurance plans, but may not determine their eligibility for subsidies or enroll them in plans—functions that are left to the exchanges. A variety of organizations may become navigators, including labor unions, trade associations, chambers of commerce, and other entities. Navigators may not be health insurers or take compensation from insurers for selling health policies. Navigators must have 20 hours of training on consumer privacy, exchange-based insurance offerings, and other issues. HHS has provided about $60 million in yearly grants for navigators at federally financed and state partnership exchanges. In addition, HHS has determined that state-based exchanges may use ACA exchange establishment funds to create parallel, in-person, non-navigator assistance programs that perform the same function as navigators. Exchanges must also certify "certified application counselors" to help with outreach and enrollment, though no new ACA funds are available for such programs.

Consumers and small businesses may continue to use insurance brokers and agents, including web-based brokers, to compare and buy coverage, both on and off the exchanges. Brokers and agents are licensed by the states, and are generally paid on a commission basis by insurance companies. While brokers and agents may choose to become navigators, they may not accept compensation from health insurance companies in that role. Consumers may also purchase policies directly from health insurers. Outside non-profit groups and businesses, such as insurers, operate their own separate efforts to educate consumers about the ACA and the process of applying for qualified health plans (QHP) and other programs.

Some lawmakers, agents, and brokers have raised questions about the navigator and other assistance programs. Issues include whether navigators have sufficient training and whether HHS regulations provide sufficiently stringent consumer and privacy safeguards. A number of states have passed legislation to further regulate navigators, including requiring navigators to be licensed and to be liable for financial losses due to their advice. HHS has determined that the ACA gives states authority to set additional standards, so long as they do not prevent implementation of Title I of the law, which includes the exchanges and navigator program. This report describes exchange outreach programs, the role of brokers, agents, and insurers, and issues regarding consumer outreach assistance.

Contents

Tables

Appendixes

Contacts

Introduction

The 2010 Patient Protection and Affordable Care Act (ACA, P.L. 111-148 as amended) mandated the creation of state health care exchanges for the sale of insurance policies, including certain individual and small-group policies.[1] Under the ACA, a state may set up its own exchange or create an exchange in partnership with the federal government. If a state chooses not to form an exchange, or cannot meet ACA requirements, the Department of Health and Human Services (HHS) will run its exchange. (See text box below, "Glossary of ACA Terms.")

Glossary of ACA Terms

State-Based Exchange—As exchange set up and run by a state, following ACA guidelines. Can be designed as a non-profit or governmental entity. Under a state-based exchange, HHS may carry out some functions, such as reinsurance, risk adjustment, and determining eligibility for premium subsidies, and tax credits.

Federally Facilitated Exchange—If a state chooses not to operate its own exchange, or does not have approval to operate its own exchange, the Secretary of HHS is required to establish a federally facilitated exchange in the state. Either states or the federal government may perform some exchange functions such as reinsurance and determining eligibility for federal health care programs.

State Partnership Exchange—A state may enter into a "partnership" with a federally facilitated exchange, combining state-designed and -operated functions with federally designed and operated functions. Partnership exchanges are considered a subset of federally facilitated exchanges, indicating that HHS has authority over partnerships in a federally facilitated exchange. Under this arrangement, states administer and operate plan management and/or consumer assistance activities.

SHOP—Small Business Health Options Program that assists small businesses in enrolling employees in qualified health plans offered in the small-employer market. A SHOP may be part of a larger exchange or a stand-alone exchange run by the state or federal government. The SHOP exchange is responsible for collecting and verifying information from employers and employees, determining eligibility, and facilitating enrollment.

Individual Exchange—Part of a larger exchange or a stand-alone exchange where individuals may shop for qualified health plans, apply for premium subsidies, and enroll in individual health plans. Individuals will also receive assistance in determining whether they qualify for Medicaid or other government programs. May be part of a larger federal or state exchange, or a stand-alone exchange.

State-based SHOP/federally facilitated Individual Exchange—Hybrid system where a state establishes and administers a SHOP exchange and the federal government sets up and runs the individual exchange for the state.

As of July 2014, 14 states and the District of Columbia had secured HHS approval to create their own exchanges, 7 to enter into partnership exchanges, 29 to have federally facilitated exchanges, and 2 to have state-based SHOP/federally facilitated individual exchanges. The exchanges began offering insurance on October 1, 2013. The insurance policies, and the exchanges, were fully operational on January 1, 2014.[2]

An exchange is not an insurer, but is rather a type of marketplace where private insurance companies may sell qualified health plans (QHP) that meet certain federal standards.[3] Consumers,

---

[1] CRS Report R43066, *Federal Funding for Health Insurance Exchanges*, by Annie L. Mach and C. Stephen Redhead.

[2] Ibid. To qualify to use an exchange, an individual must be a citizen, national, or noncitizen who is lawfully present in the United States; must not be incarcerated, other than pending the disposition of charges; and must meet applicable state residency standards.

[3] Qualified health plans must meet ACA guidelines regarding benefits, cost-sharing and other features. Exchanges use a single application to determine eligibility for enrollment in QHPs, for federal assistance and government programs such as Medicaid, and the Children's Health Insurance Program (CHIP).

businesses, and issuers are not required to use the exchanges to purchase insurance. However, individuals must buy exchange-based coverage to qualify for federal premium tax credits and cost-sharing subsidies.[4] Small businesses that apply for coverage through the exchanges may be eligible for small business tax credits.[5] Consumers may apply for coverage over the phone, online, via mail, or in person in some areas.

The Congressional Budget Office (CBO) projects that 25 million individuals will be enrolled in health insurance through the exchanges in 2024.[6] New enrollees are expected to be poorer, more racially and ethnically diverse, less educated, and less familiar with insurance than those who currently have health insurance coverage.[7] To help these consumers negotiate the enrollment process, the ACA requires exchanges to perform education and outreach functions. Exchanges may use a variety of techniques to reach out to the public including mailings, brochures, social media, corporate partnerships, health fairs, and other public events.

Consumer Assistance Programs

Under the ACA and implementing regulations issued by the HHS Centers for Medicare & Medicaid Services (CMS), consumer assistance[8] outreach programs include the following:

---

[4] CRS Report R41137, *Health Insurance Premium Credits in the Patient Protection and Affordable Care Act (ACA)*, by Bernadette Fernandez.

[5] CRS Report R41158, *Summary of Small Business Health Insurance Tax Credit Under the Patient Protection and Affordable Care Act (ACA)*, by Annie L. Mach.

[6] Congressional Budget Office, *Updated Estimates of the Effects of the Insurance Coverage Provisions of the Affordable Care Act*, Table 2, April 2014, http://www.cbo.gov/sites/default/files/cbofiles/attachments/45231-ACA_Estimates.pdf.

[7] Testimony of Gary Cohen, Deputy Administrator and Director, Center for Consumer Information and Insurance Oversight, Centers for Medicare & Medicaid Services, House Committee on Oversight and Government Reform, May 21, 2013, http://oversight.house.gov/wp-content/uploads/2013/05/Cohen-Testimony-Final.pdf, and U.S. Census Bureau, http://www.census.gov/hhes/www/hlthins/data/incpovhlth/2011/Table7.pdf.

[8] Navigator program regulations can be found at 45 C.F.R. Part 155.210; http://www.ecfr.gov/cgi-bin/retrieveECFR?gp=1&SID=8614bcc3938647b1f40def8fc1076542&ty=HTML&h=L&r=PART&n=45y1.0.1.2.70#45:1.0.1.2.70.3.27.3. Published *Federal Register* proposals and rules include: Department of Health and Human Services, "Patient Protection and Affordable Care Act; Establishment of Exchanges and Qualified Health Plans; Proposed Rule," 45 C.F.R. Parts 144 and 145, July 15, 2011, http://www.gpo.gov/fdsys/pkg/FR-2011-07-15/pdf/2011-17610.pdf; Department of Health and Human Services, "Patient Protection and Affordable Care Act; Establishment of Exchanges and Qualified Health Plans; Exchange Standards for Employers; Final Rule and Interim Final Rule," 45 C.F.R. Parts 155, 156, and 157, March 27, 2012, http://www.gpo.gov/fdsys/pkg/FR-2012-03-27/pdf/2012-6125.pdf; Centers for Medicare & Medicaid Services, "Patient Protection and Affordable Care Act; Exchange Functions: Standards for Navigators and Non-Navigator Assistance Personnel, Proposed Rule,"45 C.F.R. Part 155, April 5, 2013, https://federalregister.gov/a/2013-07951.pdf; Centers for Medicare & Medicaid Services, "Patient Protection and Affordable Care Act; Program Integrity: Exchange, SHOP, Premium Stabilization Programs, and Market Standards; Proposed Rule," 45 C.F.R. Parts 144, 147, 153, et al., June 19, 2013, http://www.gpo.gov/fdsys/pkg/FR-2013-06-19/pdf/2013-14540.pdf; Centers for Medicare & Medicaid Services, "Patient Protection and Affordable Care Act; Centers for Medicare & Medicaid Services, "Children's Health Insurance Programs, and Exchanges: Essential Health Benefits in Alternative Benefit Plans, Eligibility Notices, Fair Hearing and Appeal Processes for Medicaid and Exchange Eligibility Appeals and Other Provisions Related to Eligibility and Enrollment for Exchanges, Medicaid and CHIP, and Medicaid Premiums and Cost Sharing, Final Rule," 42 C.F.R. Parts 430, 431, 433,et al., 45 C.F.R. Part 155, pp. 42159-42322, July 15, 2013, http://www.gpo.gov/fdsys/pkg/FR-2013-07-15/pdf/2013-16271.pdf; Centers for Medicare & Medicaid Services, "Patient Protection and Affordable Care Act; Exchange Functions: Standards for Navigators and Non-Navigator Assistance Personnel, Consumer Assistance Tools and Programs of an Exchange and Certified Application Counselors, Final Rule,"45 C.F.R. Part 155, July 17, 2013, http://www.gpo.gov/

(continued...)

- Mandatory navigator programs[9] designed to provide "fair and impartial" information about exchange-based insurance plans, as well as the availability of federal assistance to help defray the cost of insurance and other health programs.

- Non-navigator or "in-person assistance" programs at state-run exchanges and state partnership exchanges.[10] The non-navigators perform generally the same functions as navigators,[11] or complement the role of navigators by reaching out to underserved populations, but have a separate source of federal funding via exchange establishment grants. Non-navigators are optional at state exchanges, and mandatory at certain partnership exchanges.

- Certified application counselors to help individuals apply for QHP enrollment and possible subsidies.[12] Exchanges may designate various organizations or individuals as application counselors or allow outside organizations to certify the counselors. Counselors are mandatory, but their duties are more limited than those of navigators and non-navigators. No new ACA funds were provided for the counselors, though they may be funded through existing state, local, or federal programs.

In addition, consumers and businesses may use insurance brokers and agents, including web-based brokers (where allowed by states), to purchase QHPs.[13] Brokers and agents, licensed by states, are generally paid a commission by insurance companies for selling their policies. Brokers and agents may apply to serve as navigators, but may not accept direct or indirect compensation from health or stop-loss insurers in this role.

Under CMS rules, consumers may also go directly to insurance companies to obtain information about QHPs and other insurance options, and to sign up for such plans.[14]

(...continued)

fdsys/pkg/FR-2013-07-17/pdf/2013-17125.pdf; and Centers for Medicare & Medicaid Services, "Patient Protection and Affordable Care Act; Program Integrity: Exchange, SHOP, and Eligibility Appeals; Final Rule," 45 C.F.R. Parts 147, 153, 155. et al., August 30, 2013, http://www.gpo.gov/fdsys/pkg/FR-2013-08-30/pdf/2013-21338.pdf; and Centers for Medicare & Medicaid Services, Patient Protection and Affordable Care Act; Exchange and Insurance Market for 2015 and Beyond; Final Rule," 45 C.F.R. Parts 144, 146, 147, May 27, 2014, http://www.gpo.gov/fdsys/pkg/FR-2014-05-27/pdf/2014-11657.pdf.

[9] ACA, Section 1311.

[10] 45 C.F.R. 155.205(d) and (e) provide that each Exchange must conduct consumer assistance, outreach, and education activities, including the navigator program. According to CMS, establishing a non-Navigator consumer assistance program pursuant to 155.205(d) and (e) will help ensure that an exchange is reaching as broad a range of consumers as possible. See also Centers for Medicare & Medicaid Services, "Patient Protection and Affordable Care Act; Exchange Functions: Standards for Navigators and Non-Navigator Assistance Personnel, Consumer Assistance Tools and Programs of an Exchange and Certified Application Counselors, Final Rule," 45 C.F.R. Part 155, *Federal Register*, July 17, 2013, http://www.gpo.gov/fdsys/pkg/FR-2013-07-17/pdf/2013-17125.pdf.

[11] Centers for Medicare & Medicaid Services, "Helping Consumers Apply & Enroll Through the Marketplace," July 2013, http://www.cms.gov/CCIIO/Resources/Files/Downloads/marketplace-ways-to-help.pdf.

[12] 45 C.F.R. 155.225.

[13] 45 C.F.R. 155.220. See also Department of Health and Human Services, Center for Consumer Information and Insurance Oversight, "Role of Agents, Brokers, and Web-Brokers in Health Insurance Marketplaces," May 1, 2013, http://www.healthreformgps.org/wp-content/uploads/agent-broker-5-2.pdf.

[14] Centers for Medicare & Medicaid Services, "Patient Protection and Affordable Care Act; Program Integrity: Exchange, SHOP, and Eligibility Appeals; Final Rule,", 45 C.F.R. Parts 147, 153, 155. et al., *Federal Register*, August 30, 2013, http://www.gpo.gov/fdsys/pkg/FR-2013-08-30/pdf/2013-21338.pdf.

Some lawmakers, as well as brokers and agents, have questioned whether CMS regulations impose sufficient training and consumer safeguards for the navigator, non-navigator, and consumer assistance programs. A number of states have passed legislation to require navigators to have additional training and licensing, or to undergo background checks.[15] The ACA gives states flexibility to certify or license navigators, but state actions may not prevent the implementation of Title I of the ACA, which authorizes the exchanges. CMS has interpreted the law to mean that states may not require all navigators, for example, to be licensed as insurance agents or brokers.[16] (See "State and Exchange Licensing and Certification.") This report outlines federal and state oversight of navigators, the role of brokers and agents, and previous education and outreach efforts for federal health care programs.

Navigator Program

The navigator program is described in Section 1311(i) of the ACA. Exchanges are required to have navigators who will perform duties that include

- conducting public education activities to raise awareness of the availability of QHPs;

- distributing fair and impartial information concerning enrollment in QHPs, and the availability of premium tax credits and cost-sharing assistance;

- facilitating enrollment in QHPs;

- referring any enrollee with a grievance, complaint, or question regarding a health plan to an applicable office of health insurance consumer assistance, a health insurance ombudsman, or any other appropriate state agency or agencies; and

- providing information that is culturally and linguistically appropriate to the population being served by the exchange.

The ACA directed the Secretary of HHS (Secretary) to establish standards for the navigator program, in collaboration with states. The Secretary is to ensure that navigators are qualified and licensed, if appropriate, and to set standards to avoid conflicts of interest in the program.

CMS regulations to implement the ACA specify that navigators may offer consumers assistance in comparing and analyzing insurance options, but may not tell applicants which health plan to select. In addition, exchanges, rather than navigators, formally determine whether an applicant is eligible for tax credits and other assistance to defray the cost of health coverage. Exchanges also formally enroll applicants into QHPs, with some exceptions.[17]

---

[15] *Associated Press*, "Missouri Governor Vetoes Health Navigator Limits," July 8, 2014, http://www.modernhealthcare.com/article/20140708/INFO/307089976.

[16] Centers for Medicare & Medicaid Services, "Patient Protection and Affordable Care Act; Exchange Functions: Standards for Navigators and Non-Navigator Assistance Personnel, Consumer Assistance Tools and Programs of an Exchange and Certified Application Counselors, Final Rule," 45 C.F.R. Part 155, *Federal Register*, p. 42831, July 17, 2013, http://www.gpo.gov/fdsys/pkg/FR-2013-07-17/pdf/2013-17125.pdf; and Centers for Medicare & Medicaid Services, Patient Protection and Affordable Care Act; Exchange and Insurance Market for 2015 and Beyond; Final Rule," 45 C.F.R. Parts 144, 146, 147, *Federal Register*, May 27, 2014, http://www.gpo.gov/fdsys/pkg/FR-2014-05-27/pdf/2014-11657.pdf.

[17] Centers for Medicare & Medicaid Services, "Patient Protection and Affordable Care Act; Exchange Functions: Standards for Navigators and Non-Navigator Assistance Personnel," 45 C.F.R. Part 155, *Federal Register*, p. 20583, (continued...)

Eligibility to Become a Navigator

The ACA includes a list of organizations and individuals eligible to become navigators, including trade, industry, and professional associations; commercial fishing industry organizations; ranching and farming organizations; community and consumer-focused non-profit groups; chambers of commerce; unions; small business development centers; and licensed insurance agents and brokers.[18] The list is illustrative rather than definitive, and other organizations may apply for navigator status. At least one navigator for each exchange must be from a community, non-profit organization.[19]

Under the ACA, a navigator may not be a health insurer or receive direct or indirect consideration from a health insurer in connection with enrolling individuals or employees in QHPs or non-QHPs.[20] CMS regulations further bar individuals or organizations from serving as navigators if they are issuers of stop loss insurance and their subsidiaries; associations that include members of or that lobby for the insurance industry; or entities that receive direct or indirect consideration from a health insurance or stop loss insurance issuer in connection with enrolling individuals or workers in a QHP or non-QHP.[21] Stop loss insurance is a type of insurance that takes effect after a company or issuer has paid out a certain level of health care claims. Entities that self-insure (finance their own health insurance plans) often use stop-loss coverage to limit their expenses.[22]

Insurance brokers and agents may apply to become navigators, but under CMS rules they may not accept compensation from health or stop loss insurers in this role. (See "Brokers and Agents.") However, a health care provider is not barred from becoming a navigator solely because it receives payment from a health insurance issuer for providing services.[23]

(...continued)

April 5, 2013, https://federalregister.gov/a/2013-07951. The exchanges verify information regarding citizenship or immigration status, residency, income, and other factors affecting enrollee eligibility. In certain cases agents and insurance firms may enroll individuals "as through an exchange."

[18] ACA, Section 1311, http://www.gpo.gov/fdsys/pkg/BILLS-111hr3590enr/pdf/BILLS-111hr3590enr.pdf.

[19] 45 C.F.R. 155.210(c)(2). See Department of Health and Human Services, "Patient Protection and Affordable Care Act; Establishment of Exchanges and Qualified Health Plans; Exchange Standards for Employers; Final Rule and Interim Final Rule," 45 C.F.R. Parts 155, 156, and 157, *Federal Register*, March 27, 2012, p. 18332, http://www.gpo.gov/fdsys/pkg/FR-2012-03-27/pdf/2012-6125.pdf.

[20] 45 C.F.R. 155.215. See Centers for Medicare & Medicaid Services, "Patient Protection and Affordable Care Act; Exchange Functions: Standards for Navigators and Non-Navigator Assistance Personnel, Consumer Assistance Tools and Programs of an Exchange and Certified Application Counselors, Final Rule," 45 C.F.R. Part 155, *Federal Register*, pp. 42831-42833, July 17, 2013, http://www.gpo.gov/fdsys/pkg/FR-2013-07-17/pdf/2013-17125.pdf. Consideration is defined to include any monetary or nonmonetary commission, kick-back, salary, hourly wage or payment made directly or indirectly to the entity or individual from an insurance company. Examples could include free travel, gifts or other items for steering consumers to a particular health plan.

[21] Centers for Medicare & Medicaid Services, "Patient Protection and Affordable Care Act; Exchange Functions: Standards for Navigators and Non-Navigator Assistance Personnel, Consumer Assistance Tools and Programs of an Exchange and Certified Application Counselors, Final Rule," 45 C.F.R. Part 155, *Federal Register*, July 17, 2013, pp. 42831-42833, http://www.gpo.gov/fdsys/pkg/FR-2013-07-17/pdf/2013-17125.pdf.

[22] Ibid. The rules bar an issuer of stop-loss insurance, a subsidiary of a stop-loss company, or an individual or entity that receives direct or indirect consideration from a stop-loss insurer for enrolling people in health insurance plans. CMS says that a navigator should not have a personal interest in whether a small employer chooses to self-insure its employees, or chooses to enroll in fully funded insurance coverage inside or outside an exchange.

[23] Centers for Medicare & Medicaid Services, Patient Protection and Affordable Care Act; Exchange and Insurance Market for 2015 and Beyond; Final Rule," 45 C.F.R. Parts 144, 146, 147, *Federal Register*, May 27, 2014, http://www.gpo.gov/fdsys/pkg/FR-2014-05-27/pdf/2014-11657.pdf; and 45 C.F.R. 155.210(d)(4). The rules also apply (continued...)

In instances when a state operates a SHOP exchange, but that state's individual exchange is run by the federal government, CMS will allow two separate navigator programs. Such states will have a federal navigator program for the individual exchange, and a state navigator program for the SHOP. SHOP navigators could fulfill their obligation to facilitate enrollment, and refer consumers with complaints or questions to applicable government offices, by referring small businesses to agents and brokers for this type of assistance, so long as applicable state law permits agents and brokers to carry out these functions.[24]

Navigators must maintain a physical presence in their exchange service area. Navigators working for federally facilitated exchanges are not required to have their principal place of business in the exchange service area, however.[25]

Navigator Application Process

CMS in April 2013 released its initial cooperative agreement funding application[26] for individuals and organizations seeking to become navigators at federally facilitated and partnership exchanges. On August 15, 2013, CMS awarded $67 million in 12-month grants to 105 navigator organizations.[27] The grants expire in August 2014. (See "Navigator and Non-navigator Funding.") In June 2014, CMS released a funding application for $60 million in new 12-month grants for navigators in federally facilitated and state partnership exchanges. The grants are to be awarded, and take effect, in September 2014.[28]

Organizations and individuals that apply for the navigator program are required to submit certain information to CMS, including[29]

- a plan for carrying out outreach and education activities specified in the ACA and in CMS regulations;

(...continued)

to non-navigators and certified application counselors.

[24] Centers for Medicare & Medicaid Services, "Patient Protection and Affordable Care Act; Program Integrity: Exchange, SHOP, and Eligibility Appeals; Final Rule," 45 C.F.R. Parts 147, 153, 155. et al., *Federal Register*, August 30, 2013, p. 54117, http://www.gpo.gov/fdsys/pkg/FR-2013-08-30/pdf/2013-21338.pdf; and 45 C.F.R. 155.705(d).

[25] Centers for Medicare & Medicaid Services, "Patient Protection and Affordable Care Act; Exchange and Insurance Market for 2015 and Beyond; Final Rule," 45 C.F.R. Parts 144, 146, 147, *Federal Register*, May 27, 2014, http://www.gpo.gov/fdsys/pkg/FR-2014-05-27/pdf/2014-11657.pdf. See also 45 C.F.R. 155.210(e)(7).

[26] Centers for Medicare & Medicaid Services, Navigator Funding Application, "PPHF–2013–Cooperative Agreement to Support Navigators in Federally-facilitated and State Partnership Exchanges," April 9, 2013, http://apply07.grants.gov/apply/opportunities/instructions/oppCA-NAV-13-001-cfda93.750-cidCA-NAV-13-001-017645-instructions.pdf.

[27] Centers for Medicare & Medicaid Services, "New Resources Available to Help Consumers Navigate the Health Insurance Marketplace," August 15, 2013, http://www.cms.gov/Newsroom/MediaReleaseDatabase/Press-Releases/2013-Press-Releases-Items/2013-08-15 html.

[28] Centers for Medicare & Medicaid Services, "CMS Announces Opportunity to Apply for Navigator Grants in Federally-facilitated and State Partnership Marketplaces," June 10, 2014, http://www.cms.gov/Newsroom/MediaReleaseDatabase/Press-releases/2014-Press-releases-items/2014-06-10.html; and Centers for Medicare &Medicaid Services, Center for Consumer Information and Insurance Oversight, "Cooperative Agreement to Support Navigators in Federally-facilitated and State Partnership Marketplaces," June 10, 2014.

[29] Ibid.

- a description of existing relationships with employers and employees, consumers (including uninsured and underinsured consumers), or self-employed individuals likely to be eligible to enroll in a qualified health plan; or a description of how such relationships could be readily established;

- a statement attesting that the applicant is not ineligible for the program due to a financial or other relationship with health insurers;

- a plan to perform the statutory and regulatory duties of a navigator for the entire length of the agreement;

- an attestation that staff and volunteers will remain free of conflicts of interest while acting as a navigator;

- a plan to ensure that staff and volunteers complete all required training; and

- a plan to comply with data privacy and security standards.

Navigator applications are evaluated on criteria that include the scope of their planned activities; their planned budget; their background and experience; and their expertise in health issues, outreach, and working with underserved and vulnerable populations. Navigators must provide weekly, monthly, quarterly and final reports on their work, and comply with CMS evaluations. While navigator organizations are not required to perform background checks on their staff, navigator applications that do have a plan for background checks may receive a higher score on their grant application.[30]

Non-navigator/Assister Programs

CMS allows, but does not require, state-based exchanges to establish non-navigator or assister programs that perform the same basic functions as navigators.[31] States that have entered into consumer partnership exchanges[32] are required as a condition of the partnership to create non-navigator programs, in addition to their navigator programs. State-based exchanges, and states in consumer partnership exchanges, may use ACA Section 1311 exchange establishment grants for non-navigator programs during their first year of operation.[33] The ACA prohibits exchanges from

---

[30] Centers for Medicare &Medicaid Services, Center for Consumer Information and Insurance Oversight, "Cooperative Agreement to Support Navigators in Federally-facilitated and State Partnership Marketplaces," June 10, 2014, p. 28.

[31] For a discussion of non-navigator programs see Centers for Medicare & Medicaid Services, "Patient Protection and Affordable Care Act; Exchange Functions: Standards for Navigators and Non-Navigator Assistance Personnel, Proposed Rule," 45 C.F.R. Part 155, *Federal Register*, April 5, 2013, p. 20583, https://federalregister.gov/a/2013-07951.pdf; and Centers for Medicare & Medicaid Services, "Patient Protection and Affordable Care Act; Exchange Functions: Standards for Navigators and Non-Navigator Assistance Personnel, Consumer Assistance Tools and Programs of an Exchange and Certified Application Counselors, Final Rule," 45 C.F.R. Part 155, *Federal Register*, July 17, 2013, p. 42825, http://www.gpo.gov/fdsys/pkg/FR-2013-07-17/pdf/2013-17125.pdf.

[32] Ibid. In a consumer partnership exchange, a state is responsible for the day-to-day management of the exchange navigators and the development and management of a separate in-person assistance program, and can choose to be responsible for outreach and educational activities. HHS will operate the exchange call center and website and be responsible for the funding and award of navigator grants. Centers for Medicare & Medicaid Services, "Guidance on State Partnership Exchange," January 3, 2013, http://www.cms.gov/CCIIO/Resources/Fact-Sheets-and-FAQs/Downloads/partnership-guidance-01-03-2013.pdf. A partnership exchange is a second type of partnership. In this type of exchange, states assume primary plan management responsibility.

[33] Centers for Medicare & Medicaid Services, "Patient Protection and Affordable Care Act; Exchange Functions: Standards for Navigators and Non-Navigator Assistance Personnel, Consumer Assistance Tools and Programs of an (continued...)

---

using Section 1311 exchange establishment grants for regular navigator programs, with some limited exceptions.

Table 1. Types of Consumer Assistance Available at Exchanges

	Location	Funding
Navigators	All exchanges.	Funded through state and federal grant programs.
In-Person Assisters/Non-Navigators	Optional for state-based exchange, Mandatory for consumer partnership exchange.	Funded through separate ACA grants or by states.
Certified Application Counselors	All exchanges.	May be funded through existing state, federal, and other programs.
Agents and Brokers	All exchanges, if allowed by states.	Compensated by insurers.

Source: Centers for Medicare & Medicaid Services.

Notes: Agents and brokers may serve as navigators if they agree not to take any compensation from health insurers for insurance sales and also meet other standards.

CMS created the non-navigator program to address the possibility that some exchanges might not have sufficient money for education and outreach during their early months of operation. State-based exchanges can use non-navigators to fill in any gaps in their navigator programs, and provide a full range of services during their first year.[34] Possible funding for following years is not clear. The ACA requires that each exchange be self-sustaining, beginning January 1, 2015. The ACA provides that an exchange may charge an assessment or user fee to participating issuers, but also allows an exchange to find other ways to generate funds to sustain its operations, which include continuing education and outreach activities.[35]

Like navigators, non-navigators may not be issuers of health insurance and their subsidiaries, including stop-loss insurance; associations that include members of or that lobby for the insurance industry; or entities that receive direct or indirect consideration from a health insurance or stop-loss insurance issuer in connection with enrolling individuals or workers in a QHP or non-QHP. Non-navigator programs at consumer partnership exchanges, and state-based exchanges funded through ACA exchange grants, are subject to the same training and conflict-of-interest restrictions as navigators.[36] State-based exchanges that create non-navigator programs with their own money, rather than with exchange establishment funds, are encouraged, but not required, to use CMS navigator standards. Non-navigators in federally funded exchanges and state exchanges must maintain a physical presence in the exchange areas. Non-navigators in federally funded exchanges do not have to have their principal place of business in the exchange area.[37]

(...continued)

Exchange and Certified Application Counselors, Final Rule," 45 C.F.R. Part 155, *Federal Register*, p. 42825, July 17, 2013, http://www.gpo.gov/fdsys/pkg/FR-2013-07-17/pdf/2013-17125.pdf.

[34] A state-run exchange may set up or continue to operate a non-navigator program from its own funds after its first year of operation to supplement its fully funded navigator program.

[35] CRS Report R43066, *Federal Funding for Health Insurance Exchanges*, by Annie L. Mach and C. Stephen Redhead.

[36] 45 C.F.R. 155.215. See also Centers for Medicare & Medicaid Services, "Patient Protection and Affordable Care Act; Exchange Functions: Standards for Navigators and Non-Navigator Assistance Personnel, Consumer Assistance Tools and Programs of an Exchange and Certified Application Counselors, Final Rule," 45 C.F.R. Part 155, *Federal Register*, July 17, 2013, http://www.gpo.gov/fdsys/pkg/FR-2013-07-17/pdf/2013-17125.pdf. Non-navigator programs are also called in-person assistance programs.

[37] 45 C.F.R. 155.215(h).

State-run exchanges have some flexibility in defining the roles of in-person assistance or non-navigator personnel and determining how their duties mesh with those of the navigators. For example, states can require non-navigators to target different demographic groups or perform different functions than navigators.[38]

Certified Application Counselors

CMS regulations require state exchanges to have certified application counselor programs to help facilitate enrollment in QHPs.[39] There is no new federal funding for the counselors, though state-based exchanges may use Section 1311 establishment funds for counselor training.[40] Exchanges are not prohibited from using existing private, state, or federal programs to fund the counselors.

Federally facilitated exchanges may designate organizations to certify their staff or volunteers to perform as certified application counselors. Exchanges must focus on organizations that already have systems in place for protecting personally sensitive data, such as state Medicaid and CHIP agencies, hospitals and other health care providers, or social service agencies.[41] State-based marketplaces may designate outside organizations to certify staff and volunteers as application counselors, or may directly certify application counselors.[42]

Like navigators and non-navigators, certified application counselors are to provide information regarding the full range of QHPs offered at an exchange and health insurance affordability programs. The counselors must work "in the best interest" of enrollees when helping individuals and employees apply for QHPs and other coverage.[43] Counselors must go through exchange-approved training and comply with data security and privacy standards and applicable state and federal laws.[44] They may work through an exchange or navigators and non-navigators to provide appropriate services to people with disabilities or to address complaints, grievances, and other questions.[45] Certified application counselors must be recertified on at least an annual basis and

---

[38] Kaiser Family Foundation, "Navigator and In-Person Assistance Programs: A Snapshot of State Programs," April 2013, http://kaiserfamilyfoundation files.wordpress.com/2013/04/8437.pdf.

[39] 45 C.F.R. 155.225, Centers for Medicare & Medicaid Services, "Patient Protection and Affordable Care Act; Exchange Functions: Standards for Navigators and Non-Navigator Assistance Personnel, Consumer Assistance Tools and Programs of an Exchange and Certified Application Counselors, Final Rule," 45 C.F.R. Part 155, *Federal Register*, p. 42824 and 42828, July 17, 2013, http://www.gpo.gov/fdsys/pkg/FR-2013-07-17/pdf/2013-17125.pdf. Helping to facilitate enrollment means helping consumers with application forms, clarifying differences among QHPs, and helping a qualified individual decide on a plan.

[40] Ibid.

[41] Centers for Medicare & Medicaid Services, "Guidance on Certified Application Counselor Program for the Federally-Facilitated Marketplace including State Partnership Marketplaces," July 12, 2013, http://www.cms.gov/CCIIO/Resources/Regulations-and-Guidance/Downloads/CAC-guidance-7-12-2013.pdf.

[42] Centers for Medicare & Medicaid Services, "Helping Consumers Apply & Enroll through the Marketplace," http://www.cms.gov/CCIIO/Resources/Files/Downloads/marketplace-ways-to-help.pdf.

[43] 45 C.F.R. Part 155.225 (c).

[44] Ibid.

[45] Centers for Medicare & Medicaid Services, "Patient Protection and Affordable Care Act; Exchange Functions: Standards for Navigators and Non-Navigator Assistance Personnel, Consumer Assistance Tools and Programs of an Exchange and Certified Application Counselors, Final Rule," 45 C.F.R. Part 155, *Federal Register*, July 17, 2013, p. 42825, http://www.gpo.gov/fdsys/pkg/FR-2013-07-17/pdf/2013-17125.pdf. In addition, exchanges, rather than counselors, would refer enrollees to other state or federal programs, to help them with grievances or complaints regarding health coverage.

---

must meet any licensing, certification, or other standards set by a state or exchange, so long as the standards do not prevent the implementation of the ACA.[46]

Certified application counselors may not receive consideration directly or indirectly from any health insurance issuer or issuer of stop-loss insurance in connection with the enrollment of any individual in a QHP or a non-QHP.[47] Health providers or other entities may not be disqualified from becoming certified application counselors solely because they receive payment from a health insurer for providing health care services.[48] Certified application counselors do not have to maintain a physical place of business in the exchange area, and counselors working for a federally funded exchange do not have to have their principal place of business in the exchange area.[49]

Federally Qualified Health Centers

CMS in 2013 provided $150 million in grants to more than 1,100 community health centers, which may serve as application counselors, to help enroll consumers in QHPs.[50] CMS provided an additional $58 million to the health centers in December 2013 to help during final enrollment.[51]

Conflict-of-Interest Rules

Navigators and non-navigators funded through Section 1311 exchange establishment funding must attest that they are eligible entities and submit a written plan to remain free of conflicts while serving in these roles.[52]

CMS regulations (45 C.F.R. 155.215) state that certain business arrangements or relationships are not necessarily a bar to serving as a navigator or a non-navigator, so long as they do not prevent an entity from providing information and services in a fair, accurate, and impartial manner. To mitigate possible conflicts of interest, CMS requires covered navigators and non-navigators to reveal certain information regarding possible conflicts of interest to exchanges and consumers.

Additional information to be disclosed[53] includes background about

- any lines of insurance, other than health care or stop loss coverage, that a navigator intends to sell while serving as a navigator;

---

[46] 45 C.F.R. 155.225.

[47] 45 C.F.R. 155.225(g)(2).

[48] May 27 FR, p. 30323, C.F.R. 155.225.

[49] 45 C.F.R. 155.225(b)(3).

[50] Department of Health and Human Services, "Health Centers to Help Uninsured Individuals Gain Affordable Health Insurance Coverage," May 9, 2013, http://www.hhs.gov/news/press/2013pres/05/20130509a html#.UgQP88q2rz4.

[51] Department of Health and Human Services, "Health Centers to Help Uninsured Americans Gain Affordable Health Insurance Coverage," December 11, 2013, http://www.hhs.gov/news/press/2013pres/12/20131211b html.

[52] 45 C.F.R. 155.215, Centers for Medicare & Medicaid Services, "Patient Protection and Affordable Care Act; Exchange Functions: Standards for Navigators and Non-Navigator Assistance Personnel, Consumer Assistance Tools and Programs of an Exchange and Certified Application Counselors, Final Rule," 45 C.F.R. Part 155, *Federal Register*; July 17, 2013, p. 42833, http://www.gpo.gov/fdsys/pkg/FR-2013-07-17/pdf/2013-17125.pdf.

[53] Ibid.

- any existing and former employment relationship during the past five years with an issuer of health or stop-loss insurance or a subsidiary;

- any existing employment relationship between any issuer of health care or stop loss insurance and an individual's spouse or domestic partner; and

- any existing or anticipated financial, business, or contractual relationships with one or more issuers of health or stop-loss insurance or their subsidiaries.

If an entity or organization is awarded a navigator or non-navigator grant, conflict-of-interest rules apply to its entire staff. Certified application counselors must disclose potential conflicts of interest either to an exchange or an exchange-designated organization.[54]

Exchange Standards

In May 2014 CMS issued final rules designed to further protect enrollees and prevent possible abuse in outreach and enrollment activities. The rules require navigators, non-navigators, and certified application counselors to ensure that applicants are informed of the functions and responsibilities of navigators and other assistance personnel. In addition, they must obtain authorization from a consumer prior to obtaining access to the consumer's personally identifiable information and maintain a record of the authorization.[55] A consumer may revoke the authorization at any time.[56]

In addition, the final rules state that navigators, non-navigators and certified application counselors

- May not be compensated by their organizations on a per-application, per-individual assistance, or per-enrollment basis. The provision, which takes effect on November 15, 2014, applies to federally funded exchanges.[57]

- May not charge any applicant or enrollee, or request or receive any form of remuneration from or on behalf of an individual applicant or enrollee, for assistance related to assister duties.[58]

- May not provide gifts, gift cards, or cash of more than nominal value ($15) or items of any value that market or promote products or services of a third party.[59] (Gifts, gift cards, or cash that exceed nominal value may be used to reimburse

---

[54] 45 C.F.R. 155.225(d)(2). Centers for Medicare & Medicaid Services, "Patient Protection and Affordable Care Act; Exchange Functions: Standards for Navigators and Non-Navigator Assistance Personnel, Consumer Assistance Tools and Programs of an Exchange and Certified Application Counselors, Final Rule," 45 C.F.R. Part 155, *Federal Register*, pp. 42825-42826, July 17, 2013, http://www.gpo.gov/fdsys/pkg/FR-2013-07-17/pdf/2013-17125.pdf.

[55] Assisters such as navigators and non-navigators are required to keep a record of the authorization. In a federally financed exchange, the record must be retained for a minimum of six years.

[56] Ibid, p. 6 and 45 C.F.R. 155.215.

[57] 45 C.F.R. 155.215(i) and 155.225(g)(3). The provision applies to federally funded exchanges. Assisters operating in SHOP exchanges are not subject to the rule, though CMS will evaluate and monitor the exchanges.

[58] 45 C.F.R. 155.210(d)(5), 155.215(a)(2)(i), and 155.225(g)(1).

[59] 45 C.F.R. 155.210(d)(6), 155.215(a)(2)(i), and 155.225(g)(4).

applicants for legitimate expenses incurred while seeking assistance through an exchange, such as postage or travel expenses.)[60]

- May not solicit consumers for application or enrollment assistance by going door-to-door or through other direct contact such as a phone call, unless the consumer initiates contact or has a preexisting relationship with the assister organization and other applicable state and federal laws are complied with.[61] Outreach and education activities may be conducted by going door-to-door or through other unsolicited contact, including phone calls.

- May not use automatic telephone dialing systems or prerecorded voice messages to initiate contact with a potential enrollee unless there is a preexisting relationship with the consumer and other applicable laws are complied with.

CMS rules also allow consumers to change plans if assisters make an error in their application. (See "Special Enrollment Period.")

Special Enrollment Period

Under CMS regulations, exchanges must allow qualified individuals and enrollees to enroll in or change from one QHP to another in certain instances, such as gaining a dependent through birth or marriage or becoming a U.S. citizen.[62] In addition, an individual may change plans when:

A qualified individual's, or his or her dependent's, enrollment or non-enrollment in a QHP is unintentional, inadvertent, or erroneous and is the result of the error, misrepresentation, or inaction of an officer, employee, or agent of the Exchange or HHS, or its instrumentalities as evaluated and determined by the Exchange. In such cases, the Exchange may take such action as may be necessary to correct or eliminate the effects of such error, misrepresentation, or inaction.

Training and Certification

CMS regulations include training standards[63] for federally facilitated exchanges, including partnership exchanges, and for non-navigators at state-run exchanges funded through Section 1311 grants. The CMS training standards may also be used by state exchanges for their navigator programs and for any non-navigator programs funded outside of Section 1311 grants. State exchanges may also develop their own training, with approval by HHS.[64]

Navigator and Non-navigator Training

To be certified by an exchange, navigator and non-navigator personnel at federally facilitated exchanges, including partnership exchanges, and all federally funded non-navigators at state-based exchanges, must

---

[60] Ibid.

[61] Ibid.

[62] 45 C.F.R. 155.420, Special enrollment periods.

[63] 45 C.F.R. 155.215(b) Centers for Medicare & Medicaid Services, "Patient Protection and Affordable Care Act; Exchange Functions: Standards for Navigators and Non-Navigator Assistance Personnel, Consumer Assistance Tools and Programs of an Exchange and Certified Application Counselors, Final Rule," 45 C.F.R. Part 155, *Federal Register*, July 17, 2013, http://www.gpo.gov/fdsys/pkg/FR-2013-07-17/pdf/2013-17125.pdf.

[64] Ibid, p. 42837.

- Complete 20 hours of HHS-approved training and receive a passing score on HHS-approved exams. Annual certification or recertification is required. [65]

- Be prepared to serve both the individual and SHOP exchanges and to provide services that meet the language and cultural needs of various populations, and of disabled individuals.

CMS originally called for up to 30 hours of training, but reduced the required training to 20 hours. [66] State-run exchanges may have much more extensive training. [67]

CMS rules require that navigators and covered non-navigators undergo training that includes eligibility and enrollment rules and processes; the full range of QHPs offered at an exchange; the range of insurance options including Medicaid and CHIP and other public programs; eligibility requirements for government assistance; the tax implications of enrollment decisions; privacy and security requirements; how to appeal an enrollment decision; outreach methods; and how to work effectively with people with disabilities or limited language skills. Privacy training must include processes for safeguarding health information, income and tax information, and Social Security numbers. The CMS August 2013 *Health Insurance Marketplace Navigator Standard Operating Procedures Manual* is a guide for navigators in helping consumers. [68]

The regulations also require that navigators must develop, maintain, and regularly update a body of general knowledge about the racial, ethnic, and cultural groups in their service areas, including the primary language spoken. Navigators and non-navigators must provide information in a consumer's preferred language at no cost to the consumer, as well as auxiliary aids and services for the disabled, at no cost where necessary. [69] Navigators and non-navigators are required to recruit and promote a staff that is representative of the demographic characteristics of their service area, including the languages spoken. Navigators and non-navigators must also provide appropriate materials and assistance to individuals with disabilities.

Certified Application Counselor Training

Certified application counselors must complete and achieve a passing score on a certification exam. Training materials are more limited than for the navigator program, [70] because the counselor

---

[65] Centers for Medicare &Medicaid Services, Center for Consumer Information and Insurance Oversight, "Cooperative Agreement to Support Navigators in Federally-facilitated and State Partnership Marketplaces," June 10, 2014, p. 9.

[66] Department of Health and Human Services, "New Resources Available to Help Consumers Navigate the Health Insurance Marketplace," August 15, 2013, http://www hhs.gov/news/press/2013pres/08/20130815a html and HHS letter to Representative Fred Upton, September 9, 2013.

[67] Henry J. Kaiser Family Foundation, "Navigator and In-Person Assistance Programs: A Snapshot of State Programs," April 2013, http://www healthexchange.ca.gov/BoardMeetings/Documents/April%2023,%202013/ Reports%20and%20Research%20-%20Master_April.pdf#page=36.

[68] Centers for Medicare & Medicaid Services, *Health Insurance Marketplace Navigator Standard Operating Procedures Manual*, August 2013, http://www healthreformgps.org/wp-content/uploads/navigator-SOP-manual-8-26.pdf.

[69] 45 C.F.R. 155.215 (c 1), and Centers for Medicare & Medicaid Services, Navigator Funding Application, "PPHF–2013–Cooperative Agreement to Support Navigators in Federally-facilitated and State Partnership Exchanges," April 9, 2013, http://apply07.grants.gov/apply/opportunities/instructions/oppCA-NAV-13-001-cfda93.750-cidCA-NAV-13-001-017645-instructions.pdf.

[70] 45 C.F.R. 155.225 (d)(1), and Centers for Medicare & Medicaid Services, "Patient Protection and Affordable Care Act; Exchange Functions: Standards for Navigators and Non-Navigator Assistance Personnel, Consumer Assistance (continued...)

---

program is more limited. For example, counselors do not have to receive training regarding certain federal health programs since they will not be directly referring potential enrollees to such programs. Counselors could also refer individuals with disabilities to navigator or non-navigator programs or to an exchange call center to ensure they receive appropriate services.

Privacy Protections

CMS regulations to implement the ACA include rules and procedures designed to protect enrollee privacy (45 C.F.R. 155.260). (See the **Appendix**.) The privacy and information requirements, which are in addition to other applicable state and federal laws, generally limit the collection, use, retention, and disclosure of personally identifiable information such as Social Security numbers. CMS regulations require exchanges to include these security and privacy requirements in any contract with non-exchange entities such as navigators, brokers, and agents that

- gain access to personally identifiable information submitted to an exchange; or

- collect, use, or disclose personally identifiable information gathered directly from applicants, qualified individuals, or enrollees while that individual or entity is performing the functions outlined in the agreement with the exchange.[71]

CMS regulations also require that navigators and non-navigators receive training in privacy standards and procedures, as part of their overall training. Personnel who willingly violate exchange privacy and security policies are subject to a fine of up to $25,000 per disclosure. States may set additional eligibility criteria and background checks for navigators and non-navigators, so long as they do not prevent the application of Title I of the Affordable Care Act.

CMS has taken other actions in the case of certified application counselors.[72] Federally facilitated exchanges will only designate outside organizations that (1) have processes in place to screen their staff members and volunteers who are certified application counselors to ensure that they protect personally identifiable information, (2) engage in services that position them to help those they serve with health coverage issues, and (3) have experience providing social services to the community. The organizations must submit an application to an exchange and agree to comply with applicable rules and statutes. Exchanges can withdraw from the arrangements if outside organizations and their staff do not meet agreed terms or violate privacy standards, for example.

Brokers and agents are to comply with exchange privacy and security standards through agreements with federally facilitated exchanges. The agreements will spell out how agents and brokers may use personally identifiable information and their duties to protect such data and train staff in use of the information. They will also prohibit the use of such data for any purpose other than the specific functions in the agreement, related to exchange enrollment.[73]

(...continued)

Tools and Programs of an Exchange and Certified Application Counselors, Final Rule," 45 C.F.R. Part 155, *Federal Register*, p. 42846, July 17, 2013, http://www.gpo.gov/fdsys/pkg/FR-2013-07-17/pdf/2013-17125.pdf.

[71] Tax return information is covered by Section 6103 of the IRS Code.

[72] Centers for Medicare & Medicaid Services, "Guidance on Certified Application Counselor Program for the Federally-Facilitated Marketplace including State Partnership Marketplaces," July 12, 2013, http://www.cms.gov/CCIIO/Resources/Regulations-and-Guidance/Downloads/CAC-guidance-7-12-2013.pdf.

[73] Centers for Medicare & Medicaid Services, "Patient Protection and Affordable Care Act; Program Integrity: Exchange, SHOP, and Eligibility Appeals; Final Rule," 45 C.F.R. Parts 147, 153, 155. et al., *Federal Register*, August (continued...)

CMS will monitor federally facilitated exchanges, as well as non-exchange entities associated with the exchange, for compliance with privacy and security standards established by the exchange. In addition, the HHS will oversee and monitor state exchanges, while the state exchanges will oversee non-exchange entities required to comply with the privacy and security standards set out by a state exchange. HHS oversight may include audits, investigations, inspections, and other activities.[74]

Federally facilitated exchanges, non-exchange entities associated with federal exchanges, and state-based exchanges will be required to report any privacy or security incident or breach to HHS.[75] Non-exchange entities associated with state exchanges will be required to report incidents and breaches to a state exchange.

State and Exchange Licensing and Certification

The ACA gives states and exchanges authority to impose additional licensing, certification, or other standards for navigators.[76] The ACA also contains a provision clarifying that state laws that do not prevent implementation of Title I of the ACA (which creates the exchanges and the navigator program) are not preempted by the ACA.[77]

CMS regulations interpret the ACA to mean that licensing, certification, and other state and exchange standards apply so long as they do not prevent the application of ACA Title I.[78] Along those lines, CMS has determined that states and exchanges are prohibited from imposing any requirement that would, in effect, require all navigators to be licensed agents or brokers.[79]

(...continued)

30, 2013, p. 54080, http://www.gpo.gov/fdsys/pkg/FR-2013-08-30/pdf/2013-21338.pdf.

[74] Ibid and 45 C.F.R. 155.280.

[75] Ibid, p. 54084. While initial rules called for a security breach to be reported within an hour, CMS did not include the time limit in final rules. CMS noted that the one-hour incident response timeline has been included in all data-sharing agreements required under the ACA. According to CMS: "Because the one hour incident response timeline has been included in all the data sharing agreements required under the Affordable Care Act, we have deleted the timing for incident reporting from regulation, proposed in § 155.280(c)(3), and expect it to be addressed through separate agreement."

[76] 45 C.F.R. 155.210(c)(1)(iii), directs that, to receive a navigator grant, an entity or individual must "meet any licensing, certification or other standards prescribed by the state or exchange, if applicable."

[77] ACA, Section 1321(d). Centers for Medicare & Medicaid Services, "Patient Protection and Affordable Care Act; Exchange Functions: Standards for Navigators and Non-Navigator Assistance Personnel, Consumer Assistance Tools and Programs of an Exchange and Certified Application Counselors, Final Rule," 45 C.F.R. Part 155, *Federal Register*, July 17, 2013, http://www.gpo.gov/fdsys/pkg/FR-2013-07-17/pdf/2013-17125.pdf. CMS regulations state that holding an agent or broker license is neither necessary, nor by itself sufficient, to perform the duties of a navigator, because licenses generally do not address areas in which navigators need expertise, including public coverage options that would be available to some consumers.

[78] Ibid.

[79] 45 C.F.R. 155.210. CMS in July 2013 regulations had specified that states could not require navigators to carry errors and omission coverage, but replaced that language in May 2014 with a broader prohibition against any requirement that would in effect render all navigators in the exchange to be licensed agents and brokers. Centers for Medicare & Medicaid Services, "Patient Protection and Affordable Care Act; Exchange and Insurance Market for 2015 and Beyond; Final Rule," 45 C.F.R. Parts 144, 146, 147, *Federal Register*, May 27, 2014, p. 30322, http://www.gpo.gov/fdsys/pkg/FR-2014-05-27/pdf/2014-11657.pdf.

ACA regulations define an agent or broker as "a person or entity licensed by the State as an agent, broker, or insurance producer."[80] According to CMS, if states required that every navigator go through a specific licensing process to become an agent or broker, then agents and brokers would be the only types of navigators allowed to operate at the exchanges. That, in turn, would violate a provision of ACA rules[81] mandating that each exchange have at least two different types of navigators, including one community or consumer-focused non-profit group. The list of organizations and individuals eligible to become navigators includes chambers of commerce, unions, and health workers. (See "Eligibility to Become a Navigator.")

In May 2014, CMS issued final rules that provide additional guidance regarding potential state standards that would prevent the application of ACA Title 1.[82] State standards that would prevent application of Title 1 include, but are not limited to

- requirements that navigators and non-navigators refer consumers to other entities not required to provide fair, accurate, and impartial information;

- requirements that would prevent navigators and non-navigators from providing services to all persons to whom they are required to provide assistance;[83]

- requirements that would prevent navigators and non-navigators from providing advice regarding substantive benefits or comparative benefits of different health plans; and

- imposing standards that would, as applied or as implemented in a state, prevent the application of federal requirements applicable to navigator and non-navigators entities or individuals or applicable to the exchange's implementation of the navigator and non-navigator program.

Navigator and Non-navigator Funding

Federally facilitated exchanges and partnership exchanges use federal Prevention and Public Health Fund (PPHF) dollars for grants to navigators. CMS on August 15, 2013, awarded $67 million in 12-month grants to 105 organizations at federally facilitated and partnership exchanges. The grantees began assisting with enrollment in October 2013.[84] (See **Table 2.**)

---

[80] Department of Health and Human Services, "Patient Protection and Affordable Care Act; Establishment of Exchanges and Qualified Health Plans; Exchange Standards for Employers; Final Rule and Interim Final Rule," 45 C.F.R. Parts 155, 156, and 157, p. 18331, March 27, 2012, http://www.gpo.gov/fdsys/pkg/FR-2012-03-27/pdf/2012-6125.pdf.

[81] 45 C.F.R. 155.210(c)(2).

[82] Centers for Medicare & Medicaid Services, "Patient Protection and Affordable Care Act; Exchange and Insurance Market for 2015 and Beyond; Final Rule," 45 C.F.R. Parts 144, 146, 147, *Federal Register*, May 27, 2014, p. 30344, http://www.gpo.gov/fdsys/pkg/FR-2014-05-27/pdf/2014-11657.pdf.

[83] Regarding the first two bullets, navigators in state SHOP-only exchanges are permitted under federal law to fulfill some of their duties through referrals to agents and brokers, if state law allows.

[84] Centers for Medicare & Medicaid Services, Center for Consumer Information & Insurance Oversight, "Navigator Grant Awards" August 15, http://www.cms.gov/CCIIO/Programs-and-Initiatives/Health-Insurance-Marketplaces/Downloads/navigator-list-8-15-2013.pdf; and Navigator Funding Application, "PPHF–2013–Cooperative Agreement to Support Navigators in Federally-facilitated and State Partnership Exchanges," April 9, 2013, http://apply07.grants.gov/apply/opportunities/instructions/oppCA-NAV-13-001-cfda93.750-cidCA-NAV-13-001-017645-instructions.pdf. CMS also released a list of organizations and businesses working with HHS on outreach, in addition to other consumer assistance programs. See http://marketplace.cms.gov/help-us/champions-for-coverage-list.pdf.

CMS allocated the funding for each state based on the number of uninsured residents in the state under the age of 65 as a share of the overall number of uninsured in states with a federally facilitated or partnership exchange. The amount of funding awarded to each navigator via the application process was based on the breadth of its proposed educational and outreach activities and the size of the population to be served. Each navigator applicant was eligible for one non-renewable, one-year cooperative agreement award, though HHS may end funding early in certain cases.[85] Grantees included food banks, county commissioners, hospitals and health systems, universities, legal aid societies, Planned Parenthood chapters, a health plan for uninsured fishermen, and American Indian health services.

Table 2. 2013 Federal Navigator Grants to Top 10 States with Highest Uninsured

Grants are for programs at federally facilitated and partnership exchanges. (In millions of dollars)

State	Number of Uninsured Under Age 65	Initial Navigator Funding Allocation
Texas	4,888,650	$10.8
Florida	3,509,164	$7.8
Georgia	1,698,883	$3.8
Illinois	1,403,613	$3.1
Ohio	1,354,868	$3.0
North Carolina	1,346,601	$3.0
Pennsylvania	1,242,351	$2.7
Michigan	1,145,493	$2.5
Arizona	947,880	$2.1
Indiana	909,633	$2.0
New Jersey	901,290	$2.0

Source: CMS, Cooperative Agreement to Support Navigators in Federally-facilitated and State Partnership Exchanges. Grants are funded for a 12-month period from the date of the award.

CMS has announced a second round of navigator grants, for the 12-month period beginning in September 2014. Each participating state will be eligible for at least $600,000 in navigator funding.[86]

Section 1311 of the ACA provides indefinite (i.e., unspecified) amounts of money for planning and establishment grants for exchanges. For each fiscal year, the Secretary is to determine the total to be made available to each state for exchange grants. However, no grant may be awarded after January 1, 2015.[87] ACA Section 1311 (i)(6) prohibits exchanges from using Section 1311 establishment funds to fund navigator grants. CMS regulations allow state-based exchanges and consumer partnership exchanges to use Section 1311 exchange grants to fund non-navigator

---

[85] Ibid. p. 10. For example, a grant may end sooner than 12 months if a federally facilitated exchange or state partnership exchange is replaced by a state-based exchange. In addition, the ability of a grantee to receive quarterly funding installments depends on whether it is in compliance with the terms and conditions of the grant.

[86] Centers for Medicare & Medicaid Services, Center for Consumer Information and Insurance Oversight, "Cooperative Agreement to Support Navigators in Federally-facilitated and State Partnership Marketplaces," June 10, 2014.

[87] CRS Report R43066, *Federal Funding for Health Insurance Exchanges*, by Annie L. Mach and C. Stephen Redhead.

assistance programs during their initial year of operation.[88] Section 1311 funds may also be used to cover an exchange's cost of administering the navigator program, including training, grants management, and oversight.[89]

State-based exchanges appear to have spent more for outreach than have federally facilitated exchanges. A study of select exchanges by The Urban Institute found that state exchanges spent an average of $30.66 in outreach per beneficiary, compared to $11.49 at federally facilitated and partnership exchanges.[90] The study also found that states operating their own exchanges tended to have more stringent training requirements. Likewise, a Kaiser Family Foundation survey found that states with partnership or state-run exchanges had about twice as many assisters per 10,000 uninsured consumers as states with federally facilitated exchanges.[91]

Brokers and Agents

U.S. health insurance agents and brokers, collectively called "producers," are a contact point between insurance companies and applicants, helping individuals and businesses choose suitable policies.[92] According to the Bureau of Labor Statistics (BLS), producers selling all types of insurance, including health policies, held about 443,400 jobs in 2012 and had median annual wages of $48,150.[93] Insurance producers are a major segment of the U.S. financial services industry, offering annuity products, comprehensive financial planning services, such as retirement and estate planning, and business pension planning.[94]

Though insurance producers work with consumers, they are paid by insurance companies. An agent may be a so-called captive agent who works for one insurance firm, or an independent agent who sells products from a variety of insurers. Independent agents may be paid via commission, while those working for an agency or insurer may receive a salary, often plus commission or bonus. An insurance broker generally represents a wider array of insurance

---

[88] Centers for Medicare & Medicaid Services, "Patient Protection and Affordable Care Act; Exchange Functions: Standards for Navigators and Non-Navigator Assistance Personnel, Consumer Assistance Tools and Programs of an Exchange and Certified Application Counselors, Final Rule," 45 C.F.R. Part 155, *Federal Register*, p. 42825, July 17, 2013, http://www.gpo.gov/fdsys/pkg/FR-2013-07-17/pdf/2013-17125.pdf.

[89] Federally facilitated and partnership exchanges may use Section 1311 funds for certain functions, including some administrative costs, as outlined by CMS. See "Frequently Asked Questions on Allowable Uses of Section 1311 Funding for States in a State Partnership Marketplace or in States with a Federally-Facilitated Marketplace," http://www.cms.gov/CCIIO/Resources/Fact-Sheets-and-FAQs/spm-ffm-funding.html.

[90] Ian Hill, Margaret Wilkinson, and Bridget Courtout, The Urban Institute, "The Launch of the Affordable Care Act in Selected States: Outreach, Education, and Enrollment Assistance," March 2014, Table 2, http://www.urban.org/UploadedPDF/413039-The-Launch-of-the-Affordable-Care-Act-in-Eight-States-Outreach-Education-and-Enrollment-Assistance.pdf.

[91] Karen Pollitz, Jennifer Tolbert, and Rosa Ma, *Survey of Helath Insurance Marketplace Assister Programs: A First Look at Consumer Assistance under the Affordable Care Act*, Kaiser Family Foundation, July 2014, p. 11.

[92] CRS Report R41439, *Health Insurance Agents and Brokers in the Reformed Health Insurance Market*, by Bernadette Fernandez.

[93] U.S. Department of Labor, Bureau of Labor Standards, *2012 Occupational Outlook Handbook: Insurance Sales Agents*, http://www.bls.gov/ooh/sales/insurance-sales-agents htm#tab-1.

[94] The Dodd-Frank Wall Street Reform and Consumer Protection Act of 2010 (P.L. 111-203), expanded the federal regulatory role over other areas of the insurance industry. For more background, see CRS Report R43067, *Insurance Regulation: Issues, Background, and Legislation in the 113th Congress*, by Baird Webel.

---

products than an agent, and assumes a greater role in assessing the potential risk profile and insurance requirements of a client, including overall insurance needs and appropriate policies.

A web-based insurance broker may offer products from a variety of insurers on a central website. Potential clients enter basic information into the site, such as zip code and family size, and are then presented with an array of possible insurance plans. Shoppers can search for plans in different ways such as company name, average monthly cost, premiums, and other variables.

Licensing

With the exception of government-sponsored insurance programs (e.g., Medicare Advantage), agent and broker activity usually is regulated by the states,[95] which prohibit unfair sales practices and require producers to meet certain standards to become licensed.

The ACA includes several provisions that affect brokers and agents. In addition to the navigator/non-navigator program, the ACA's Medical Loss Ratio (MLR) provisions require certain large group health plans to spend at least 85% of revenues on benefits to enrollees, rather than administration or profits, while small group and individual plans must meet an 80% MLR requirement. Under CMS regulations, commissions and fees paid to brokers and agents are counted as insurance company administrative costs. Producers say that some insurance companies have reduced their commissions in an effort to contain administrative costs and meet the MLR requirements.[96]

Exchange Requirements

Agents and brokers play a role in selling QHPs to both individuals and small businesses. CMS regulations[97] were designed to allow exchanges to "leverage the market presence of agents and brokers ... to draw consumers to the Exchange and to QHPs." Exchanges may allow agents and brokers to help individuals enroll directly through an exchange website, or through outside issuer web sites, so long as they meet certain exchange standards and safeguards. Brokers or agents that discover that a potential client is qualified for federal health programs, such as Medicaid or CHIP, are expected to direct them to the appropriate public agency for assistance.[98]

---

[95] For more information on Medicare oversight of producers see Centers for Medicare and Medicaid Services, "Chapter 3 – Medicare Marketing Guidelines For Medicare Advantage Plans, Medicare Advantage Prescription Drug Plans, Prescription Drug Plans, and Section 1876 Cost Plans," June 17, 2014, http://www.cms.gov/Medicare/Health-Plans/ ManagedCareMarketing/FinalPartCMarketingGuidelines html.

[96] CRS Report R42735, *Medical Loss Ratio Requirements Under the Patient Protection and Affordable Care Act (ACA): Issues for Congress*, by Suzanne M. Kirchhoff.

[97] 45 C.F.R. 155.220. Centers for Medicare & Medicaid Services, "Patient Protection and Affordable Care Act; Establishment of Exchanges and Qualified Health Plans; Exchange Standards for Employers; Final Rule and Interim Final Rule," 45 C.F.R. Parts 155, 156, and 157, *Federal Register*, March 27, 2012, http://www.gpo.gov/fdsys/pkg/FR-2012-03-27/pdf/2012-6125.pdf; and HHS Center for Consumer Information and Insurance Oversight, "Role of Agents, Brokers, and Web-brokers in Health Insurance Marketplaces," May 1, 2013, http://www healthreformgps.org/wp-content/uploads/agent-broker-5-2.pdf.

[98] Department of Health and Human Services, Center for Consumer Information and Insurance Oversight, "Role of Agents, Brokers, and Web-Brokers in Health Insurance Marketplaces," p. 6, May 1, 2013, http://www healthreformgps.org/wp-content/uploads/agent-broker-5-2.pdf.

Federally Facilitated and Partnership Exchanges

CMS regulations set out processes for licensed agents, brokers, and web-based brokers to help consumers and employers enroll in QHPs through federally facilitated exchanges, as well as to continue to sell other, off-exchange insurance options. Federally facilitated and partnership exchanges do not pay commissions to brokers, nor do they place a cap on agent and broker commissions for selling QHPs. CMS rules do, however, require insurance companies to pay similar broker compensation for QHPs offered through such exchanges, as for similar health plans offered outside such exchanges.[99]

In states with federally facilitated or partnership exchanges, CMS requires[100] agents and brokers to register by providing proof of identity, completing an exchange-specific training course, and agreeing to comply with federal and state laws and regulations, including those regarding privacy and security.

After producers have completed the required steps and are certified by an exchange they receive an exchange user ID, which they can use, along with their national producer number, to make transactions and receive compensation from insurers.

Brokers and agents at federally facilitated and partnership exchanges can assist consumers either

- through an issuer-based pathway, using an insurer's website, or

- through an exchange pathway, with the agent or broker helping the consumer on an exchange website.

For federally facilitated SHOP exchanges, agents and brokers will use the exchange website to carry out employer and employee applications.[101]

Issuer-Based Enrollment

Since the fall of 2013, insurance agents have been allowed to assist individuals seeking QHPs by directly using insurance/issuer websites. Insurers are to assign agents and brokers to sell their products, are to check the agent or broker's license status, and are to ensure that the agent or broker is certified by an exchange.

An agent starts the signup process by logging on to an insurer's website (this is applicable in situations where the issuer has satisfied exchange requirements and has direct enrollment ability). Once a consumer is ready to apply for a QHP, the issuer website will redirect the producer and the consumer to the exchange website to complete the eligibility application. As part of the process, agents and brokers are expected to disclose to the consumer that they are providing information about QHPs for which they have a business relationship, and to tell the potential enrollee that he

---

[99] Department of Health and Human Services, Center for Consumer Information and Insurance Oversight, "Role of Agents, Brokers, and Web-Brokers in Health Insurance Marketplaces," p. 5, May 1, 2013, http://www healthreformgps.org/wp-content/uploads/agent-broker-5-2.pdf.

[100] Ibid.

[101] Centers for Medicare & Medicaid Services, "Federally-facilitated Marketplace: Agent/Broker Training Launch," August 2013, http://www.cms.gov/CCIIO/Programs-and-Initiatives/Health-Insurance-Marketplaces/Downloads/agent-broker-training-webinar.pdf.

or she may look at other QHP options on the exchange. After the consumer is verified as eligible to buy a QHP, the exchange will redirect the producer and client back to the insurer's website to compare plans and make a selection.

Exchange Website

Agents and brokers may assist consumers and qualified small employers and their employees directly on an exchange website. Agents and brokers may help consumers create exchange accounts, but the consumer (or an authorized representative) must create his or her own secure password and user name and should not share that information with third parties, including producers. When an agent uses an exchange website, all QHPs are to be displayed.

State-Based Exchanges

State-based exchanges will continue to license and regulate agents and brokers, including those who sell QHPs through the exchange. States may require continuing education or exchange-based training for producers, including state-specific training. States may implement additional requirements, such as mandating that producers provide information to consumers about all available QHPs, not just those for which they receive a commission. State-based exchanges may allow brokers and agents to be directly compensated through an exchange or through issuer-based commissions, and may allow agents and brokers to help enroll an individual in a QHP in a "manner than constitutes enrollment through the exchange."

Web-Based Brokerages

Federally facilitated and partnership exchanges are to work with web-based brokers, to the extent allowed by a state (the main entity licensing and regulating agents and brokers). While state-based marketplaces have latitude to set conditions for web-based brokers, CMS regulations require that the exchanges must perform enrollee eligibility determinations for individuals who sign up for QHPs. In addition, the state-based exchanges must transmit enrollment information to QHP issuers for all individuals enrolling through the marketplace.

CMS regulations impose additional marketing restrictions on web-based brokers to ensure, in part, that consumers do not mistake their websites for official exchange websites.[102] Web-based brokers must display available information on QHPs offered through an exchange, and provide consumers with the ability to view all exchange QHPs. Web brokers may not provide financial incentives, such as rebates or giveaways, and must allow consumers to withdraw from the application process and use the exchange website at any time.[103]

CMS will require web-based brokers to display a disclaimer including the fact that their website might not contain all QHP information available on the exchange website. Web brokers selling products offered on federally facilitated exchanges will have to use an HHS-approved disclaimer indicating that the website is not a federally facilitated exchange website, that their website might

---

[102] Centers for Medicare & Medicaid Services, "Patient Protection and Affordable Care Act; Program Integrity: Exchange, SHOP, and Eligibility Appeals; Final Rule," 45 C.F.R. Parts 147, 153, 155. et al., *Federal Register*, August 30, 2013, http://www.gpo.gov/fdsys/pkg/FR-2013-08-30/pdf/2013-21338.pdf.

[103] 45 C.F.R. 155.220.

not contain all QHP information available on the exchange website, and that the broker is subject to exchange marketing and privacy regulations. Brokers must also provide links to the appropriate exchange.[104] CMS is currently developing guidance regarding display of such disclaimers.

Direct Enrollment Through Insurers

CMS anticipates some consumers may contact insurance companies directly to enroll in QHPs. In such cases, exchanges would have the option of allowing insurers to enroll the consumers into QHPs in a manner that is considered to be enrollment through an exchange. Under CMS rules, in order for issuer enrollment to be considered as enrollment through an exchange, the insurer's website must provide applicants the option of looking at all QHPs offered by the insurer, distinguish between QHPs for which the consumer is eligible and other health plans that the insurer may offer, and make clear that the tax credits and subsidies apply only to QHPs through an exchange. The insurer must use an HHS-approved disclaimer to let consumers know of other QHPs through the exchange, as well as provide a weblink to the exchange.[105] In addition, the insurer must charge the enrollee the same premium that is charged for the QHP on an exchange, after accounting for any federal subsidy.

If permitted by an exchange, and to the extent permitted by state law, an insurer may allow its issuer application assisters[106] to help consumers apply for an eligibility determination through an exchange; apply for tax credits and other cost-sharing; and help select a QHP offered by the issuer. There must be an agreement between the insurer and the exchange under which the issuer application assisters (1) are trained in QHP options, insurance affordability programs, eligibility, and benefit rules and regulations; (2) comply with exchange privacy and security standards; and (3) comply with state laws regarding the sale, solicitation, and negotiation of health insurance products, including laws related to agent, broker, and producer licensing; confidentiality; and conflicts of interest.[107]

Previous Insurance Education and Outreach Efforts

HHS has carried out previous, major health insurance education and enrollment efforts, including enrollment efforts under the Medicare Part D prescription drug program and the Children's Health Insurance Program (CHIP). Medicare also funds the State Health Insurance Assistance Program (SHIP), which offers education and other assistance to Medicare beneficiaries and their

---

[104] Centers for Medicare & Medicaid Services, "Patient Protection and Affordable Care Act; Program Integrity: Exchange, SHOP, and Eligibility Appeals; Final Rule," 45 C.F.R. Parts 147, 153, 155. et al., *Federal Register*, August 30, 2013, p. 54078, http://www.gpo.gov/fdsys/pkg/FR-2013-08-30/pdf/2013-21338.pdf, and HHS, Center for Consumer Information and Insurance Oversight, "Role of Agents, Brokers, and Web-Brokers in Health Insurance Marketplaces," May 1, 2013, http://www.healthreformgps.org/wp-content/uploads/agent-broker-5-2.pdf. Consumers may go to the federal website Healthcare.gov for background information about the insurance exchange system.

[105] C.F.R. 156.1230 and Centers for Medicare & Medicaid Services, "Patient Protection and Affordable Care Act; Program Integrity: Exchange, SHOP, and Eligibility Appeals; Final Rule," 45 C.F.R. Parts 147, 153, 155. et al., *Federal Register*, August 30, 2013, p. 54146, http://www.gpo.gov/fdsys/pkg/FR-2013-08-30/pdf/2013-21338.pdf.

[106] 45 C.F.R. 155.20 defines an issuer application assister as an employee, contractor, or agent of a QHP issuer who is not licensed as an agent, broker, or producer under state law and who assists individuals in the individual market with applying for a determination or redetermination of eligibility for coverage through the exchange or for insurance affordability programs

[107] Ibid.

families. These efforts differ in significant ways from current, ACA outreach efforts, but have similarities including broad public relations and advertising components and extensive use of trained volunteers and community groups to help consumers make decisions about health insurance. CMS officials have looked to the programs for lessons and guidance as they launch the in-person assistance programs.

In general, government and private sector analyses of the earlier HHS efforts indicate that the most effective outreach includes a variety of techniques including distributing information via mass media; cooperation between federal and state agencies, non-profit and business organizations; and the use of community groups and individual counseling to reach low-income consumers and those with language barriers or physical disabilities.

Medicare Part D

Congress approved the voluntary, Medicare Part D prescription drug program in the Medicare Modernization Act of 2003 (MMA, P.L. 108-173). Similar to the structure of the ACA, Part D enrollees may choose from a variety of private insurance plans. An estimated 42 million Medicare beneficiaries were eligible for the initial Part D benefit. The MMA also shifted dual eligible beneficiaries—individuals who qualify for both Medicare and Medicaid—to Part D from the Medicaid program. Medicare beneficiaries were eligible to apply for a transitional, temporary drug discount card program for 2004-2005, with the full Part D benefit taking effect on January 1, 2006.

Congress provided $1 billion to implement Medicare Part D.[108] According to a GAO audit of the program, HHS used about $99 million of the $1 billion for direct outreach and education activities, including $67.3 million for materials targeted at beneficiaries and $31.6 million for efforts to reach out to Medicare providers. For example, CMS paid the public relations firm Ketchum $47.3 million for outreach initiatives including a bus tour that targeted key cities to promote the prescription drug program.[109] Other CMS spending included more than $234 million to operate a 1-800 help line to answer questions about the Part D program, according to the GAO.

As part of the overall effort, HHS, the Social Security Administration (SSA), state Medicaid programs, and other entities implemented a coordinated education and outreach campaign, focusing on low-income beneficiaries.[110] The project included distributing more than 70 written publications, creating the toll-free help line, and posting information on the Medicare website. CMS worked with coalitions that included the National Alliance for Hispanic Health, the National Association of Area Agencies on Aging, the National Council on Aging, and the Pharmaceutical Research and Manufacturers Association.[111] The Regional Education about Choice in Health

---

[108] Department of Health and Human Services, *Fiscal 2006 Budget in Brief*, p. 56, http://archive hhs.gov/budget/ 06budget/FY2006BudgetinBrief.pdf. Congress transferred $25 million of that total to the HHS Office of the Inspector General for oversight activities.

[109] Government Accountability Office, "Internal Control Deficiencies Resulted in Millions of Dollars of Questionable Contract Payments," GAO-08-54, November 2007, http://www.gao.gov/new.items/d0854.pdf. The GAO review found nearly $90 million in questionable spending.

[110] Government Accountability Office, "Medicare: Quality of CMS Communications to Beneficiaries on the Prescription Drug Benefit Could Be Improved," GAO-06-715T, May 4, 2006, http://www.gpo.gov/fdsys/pkg/ GAOREPORTS-GAO-06-715T/html/GAOREPORTS-GAO-06-715T htm.

[111] Laura Summer, Ellen O'Brien, Patricia Nemore, and Katharine Hsiao, Commonwealth Fund, "Medicare Part D: State and Local Efforts to Assist Vulnerable Beneficiaries," May 2008, http://www.commonwealthfund.org/~/media/ (continued...)

(REACH) program was aimed at beneficiaries with language, literacy, income, and other barriers to access,[112] while the Access to Benefits Coalition (ABC) was a group of nonprofits including AARP, the Salvation Army, and the American Hospital Association, and 56 local coalitions.[113] Pharmaceutical and insurance companies were active in outreach efforts, including the Medicare Rx Education Network.[114] CMS also worked through State Health Insurance and Assistance Programs (see below) and increased funding to the SHIPs to help expand outreach.[115]

Even with the coordinated efforts, millions of eligible low-income individuals did not sign up for the drug discount card, and Medicare Part D enrollment was initially less than expected. However, by 2010, 90% of those eligible had Part D drug coverage, retiree coverage subsidized by Medicare, or private coverage at least as comprehensive as the Part D benefit.[116] More than 30 million beneficiaries were enrolled in Part D plans in 2013.

State Health Insurance and Assistance Programs (SHIP)

The State Health Insurance and Assistance Program (SHIP) provides counseling and information assistance to Medicare beneficiaries and their families regarding Medicare and other health insurance issues. The SHIP is authorized under Section 4360 of the Omnibus Budget Reconciliation Act of 1990 (P.L. 101-508). Although the program's authorization of appropriations expired in FY1996, Congress continues to provide funding by transferring discretionary funding to the program from the Federal Hospital Insurance Trust Fund and the Federal Supplementary Medical Insurance Trust Fund.

Paid and volunteer SHIP counselors provide one-on-one services to Medicare beneficiaries, both in person and by telephone. There are SHIP offices in all 50 states, as well as the District of Columbia, Guam, Puerto Rico, and the Virgin Islands. Of the 54 SHIP grant programs, about two-thirds are administered by State Units on Aging established under the Older Americans Act (OAA extended by the OAA Extension of 2006, P.L. 109-365).

The more than 15,000 counselors at the 1,300 local SHIP sites serve more than 5 million consumers annually.[117]

(...continued)

Files/Publications/Issue%20Brief/2008/May/
Medicare%20Part%20D%20%20State%20and%20Local%20Efforts%20to%20Assist%20Vulnerable%20Beneficiaries/
Summer_McarePartDstatelocalefforts_1126_ib%20pdf.

[112] Government Accountability Office, "Medicare: CMS's Beneficiary Education and Outreach Efforts for the Medicare Prescription Drug Discount Card and Transitional Assistance Program," GAO-06-139R, November 30, 2005, http://www.gao.gov/assets/100/93875 html/.

[113] Ibid.

[114] *Kaiser Health News*, "Insurers, National Organizations Launch Advertising Campaigns for Medicare Rx Drug Benefit," July 20, 2005, http://www kaiserhealthnews.org/Daily-Reports/2005/July/20/dr00031514.aspx?p=1.

[115] HHS Secretary Michael Leavitt, *Report to Congress: Best Practices for Enrolling Low-Income Beneficiaries into the Medicare Prescription Drug Benefit Program*, 2009, http://www.cms.gov/Research-Statistics-Data-and-Systems/Statistics-Trends-and-Reports/Reports/downloads/Leavitt_RTC_Best_Practices_Enrolling_LI.pdf

[116] Shinobu Suzuki, "Status Report on Part D," Medicare Payment Advisory Commission," January 11, 2013, http://www medpac.gov/transcripts/status%20report%20on%20part%20D%20for%20jan%202013.pdf.

[117] Centers for Medicare & Medicaid Services, "Affordable Care Act State Health Insurance Assistance Program (SHIP) and Aging and Disability Resource Center (ADRC) Options Counseling for Medicare - Medicaid Individuals in States with Approved Financial Alignment Models," August 23, 2012, http://aoa.gov/AoARoot/Grants/Funding/docs/ (continued...)

State SHIP programs provide training for volunteers, whose duties include answering questions about Medicare, Medigap supplemental insurance, Medicare Part C, Medicare Part D, and low-income subsidies. CMS, as part of its grant making, requires SHIPs to demonstrate how their training and certification programs will ensure that counselors provide accurate information. CMS provides materials for use in creating state certification programs, and analyzes SHIP performance each year.[118] According to a recent survey of SHIP offices, initial counselor training averages 20.5 hours, and about 75% of the programs require counselors to pass a certification test.[119] CMS runs a National Medicare Training Program that assists SHIP and other volunteers.

Children's Health Insurance Program

The State Children's Health Insurance Program (CHIP) was established in the Balanced Budget Act of 1997 (BBA 97; P.L. 105-33).[120] The law was reauthorized in The Children's Health Insurance Program Reauthorization Act of 2009 (CHIPRA, P.L. 111-3). In general, CHIP allows states to cover targeted, low-income children in families with no insurance and incomes above state Medicaid limits.[121]

The BBA 97 allowed states to spend up to 10% of their initial CHIP benefit spending on administrative costs, including outreach (as opposed to 10% of the CHIP annual appropriated level). The law also permitted additional flexibility for states that expanded their Medicaid programs under CHIP. In this case, states were allowed to claim federal financial participation for administrative costs under either Medicaid or CHIP. In the Consolidated Appropriations Act of 2001 (P.L. 106-554), Congress permitted states to use up to 10% of their unspent FY1998 funds specifically for outreach activities. These outreach funds were above and beyond funding available under the existing 10% cap. There was also private funding to supplement the public outreach efforts, including funding from the Robert Wood Johnson Foundation.

Enrollment efforts included hiring outreach workers, ranging from welfare recipients to professionals and community groups, and distributing advertising and informational materials. As was the case with Part D, HHS and state Medicaid agencies worked with community groups, health care providers, and schools to contact potential beneficiaries.[122] According to the GAO,

---

(...continued)

2012/SHIP_ADRC_Duals_FOA_FINAL8_22_2012.pdf.

[118] Centers for Medicare & Medicaid Services, National SHIP Resource Center, "Evaluating Your SHIP Training and Certification Program Toolkit," August 2012, https://www.shiptalk.org/ShipTalkInfoLib/MiscDocs/OCCT_Eval_Webinar_Toolkit.pdf.

[119] Tobi Johnson and Lee Thompson, The National SHIP Resource Center, "SHIP Counselor Training and Certification Programs: Findings from a National Survey," January 2013, https://www.shiptalk.org/ShipTalkInfoLib/MiscDocs/SHIP_Training_Cert_Survey_508.pdf. The survey was distributed to the 54 state SHIP offices. Of that total, 85% answered the survey.

[120] CRS Report R40226, *P.L. 111-3: The Children's Health Insurance Program Reauthorization Act of 2009*, by Evelyne P. Baumrucker, Elicia J. Herz, and Jane G. Gravelle.

[121] Government Accountability Office, "Pre-Existing Condition Insurance Plan: Comparison of Implementation and Early Enrollment with the Children's Health Insurance Program," November 10, 2011, http://www.gao.gov/assets/590/586867.pdf. CHIP defined a targeted, low-income child as one who is under 19 years of age, with no health insurance, and who would not have been eligible for Medicaid under the rules in effect in the state on March 31, 1997.

[122] National Health Policy Forum, "CHIP and Medicaid Outreach and Enrollment: A Hands-On Look at Marketing and Applications," October 19, 1999, http://www.nhpf.org/library/issue-briefs/IB748_SCHIPOutreach_10-19-99.pdf.

---

enrollment began slowly but picked up. By the end of 2000, about three years after the law was enacted, all states had implemented their programs.

Federal agencies, including the SSA and the Departments of Agriculture, the Interior, Education, HHS, Housing and Urban Development, Labor, and the Treasury, were involved in outreach efforts. As the program progressed, states found that one-on-one efforts with community and other groups became more important in terms of connecting with hard-to-reach groups, such as immigrants and people with limited English skills.[123] States worked with an array of groups, including religious organizations, chambers of commerce, private businesses, community health centers, and education organizations not just for outreach, but to help families fill out enrollment forms and submit applications.[124] States also simplified enrollment forms, coordinated data with their Medicaid programs, and increased their use of technology to speed up the process.

CHIPRA built on this system and authorized up to $100 million in outreach and enrollment grants for fiscal years 2009 through 2013. The bulk of the authorized funds, 80%, were to be allocated to states and community-based organizations for outreach campaigns focusing on rural areas and underserved populations. The ACA expands the time period for the CHIPRA outreach and enrollment grants through 2015 and increases the appropriation level to $140 million for FY2009-FY2015.

There are some significant differences between initial CHIP enrollment and the exchange outreach effort. The scope of the CHIP target population is far smaller than the potential exchange population. In addition, the CHIP statute was not prescriptive in terms of telling states how to meet screening and enrollment requirements to determine eligibility for Medicaid and/or CHIP. States had an incentive to enroll children in CHIP, because the states were eligible for enhanced federal matching funds to expand coverage to low-income uninsured women and children, without necessarily expanding their Medicaid programs.

Outstanding Issues

Some lawmakers have raised questions and concerns about the navigator programs. Two subcommittees of the House Committee on Oversight and Investigations in May 2013 held a joint hearing on implementation of the navigator program.[125]

---

[123] Susan Williams and Margo Rosenbach, Mathematica, "Evolution of State Outreach Efforts under SCHIP," *Health Care Financing Review*, Summer 2007, pp. 95-107, http://www mathematica-mpr.com/publications/pdfs/evolutionstate.pdf

[124] Victoria Wachino and Alice Weiss, "Maximizing Kids' Enrollment in Medicaid and SCHIP," National Academy for State Health Policy, February 2009, http://nashp.org/sites/default/files/Max_Enroll_Report_FINAL.pdf?q=files/Max_Enroll_Report_FINAL.pdf.

[125] House Committee on Oversight and Government Reform, Subcommittee on Energy Policy, Health Care and Entitlements Subcommittee on Economic Growth, Job Creation and Regulatory Affairs, "Examining the Concerns about the ObamaCare Outreach Campaign Program," May 21, 2013, http://oversight.house.gov/hearing/examining-the-concerns-about-obamacare-outreach-campaign/.

Adequacy of Privacy Protections

Some Members of Congress, state legislators, health care advocacy groups, and brokers and agents have raised questions about whether CMS regulations go far enough to ensure protection of enrollees' personal information, such as Social Security numbers.

Lawmakers have asked HHS for additional information about how much access navigators, non-navigators, and certified application counselors will have to enrollees' personal information.[126] Lawmakers have asked to see specific training materials and have sought information regarding handling of documents and potential background checks of navigator personnel. A group of 13 attorneys general in an August 14, 2013 letter also raised concerns about the privacy regulations.[127]

In an effort to strengthen privacy protections, HHS in May 2014 final rules required that navigators, non-navigators, and certified application counselors obtain authorization from a consumer before accessing his or her personally identifiable information, and maintain a record of the authorization. Consumers have a right to revoke the authorization at any time.[128]

The potential for privacy violations and other consumer swindles extends well beyond exchange-sanctioned consumer assistance programs, however. The Federal Trade Commission warned consumers in 2012 about scam artists seeking to obtain personal information under the guise of verifying information regarding ACA coverage.[129]

---

[126] Letter to HHS Secretary Kathleen Sebelius, May 2013, http://waysandmeans house.gov/uploadedfiles/brady_boustany_navigator_letter_051513.pdf.

[127] Patrick Morrissey, West Virginia Attorney General, Letter to HHS Secretary Sebelius, August 14, 2013, http://www.wvago.gov/pdf/Letter%20to%20HHS%20re%20Data%20Privacy_%28final%208%2014%2013%29.pdf.

[128] 45 C.F.R. 155.210 (e) (6), 155 215.(g), and 155.225(f). See Centers for Medicare & Medicaid Services, "Patient Protection and Affordable Care Act; Exchange and Insurance Market for 2015 and Beyond; Final Rule," 45 C.F.R. Parts 144, 146, 147, *Federal Register*, May 27, 2014, http://www.gpo.gov/fdsys/pkg/FR-2014-05-27/pdf/2014-11657.pdf.

[129] Federal Trade Commission, "FTC Alert: Scammers Out to Trick Consumers Using the Supreme Court's Affordable Care Act Ruling," July 31, 2012, http://www ftc.gov/opa/2012/07/aca.shtm; Sid Kirchheimer, "New Health Benefits Scam,"AARP, March 13, 2013, http://www.aarp.org/money/scams-fraud/info-07-2012/affordable-care-act-scam.html; and Herb Weisbaum, "Beware of Obamacare Scammers," *CNBC* and *The Fiscal Times*, August 15, 2013, http://www.thefiscaltimes.com/Articles/2013/08/15/Beware-of-Obamacare-Scammers.aspx#page1.

Appendix. CMS Exchange Privacy Requirements

45 CFR § 155.260   Privacy and security of personally identifiable information.

(a) *Creation, collection, use and disclosure.* (1) Where the Exchange creates or collects personally identifiable information for the purposes of determining eligibility for enrollment in a qualified health plan; determining eligibility for other insurance affordability programs, as defined in 155.20; or determining eligibility for exemptions from the individual responsibility provisions in section 5000A of the Code, the Exchange may only use or disclose such personally identifiable information to the extent such information is necessary to carry out the functions described in § 155.200 of this subpart.

(2) The Exchange may not create, collect, use, or disclose personally identifiable information while the Exchange is fulfilling its responsibilities in accordance with § 155.200 of this subpart unless the creation, collection, use, or disclosure is consistent with this section.

(3) The Exchange must establish and implement privacy and security standards that are consistent with the following principles:

(i) *Individual access.* Individuals should be provided with a simple and timely means to access and obtain their personally identifiable information in a readable form and format;

(ii) *Correction.* Individuals should be provided with a timely means to dispute the accuracy or integrity of their personally identifiable information and to have erroneous information corrected or to have a dispute documented if their requests are denied;

(iii) *Openness and transparency.* There should be openness and transparency about policies, procedures, and technologies that directly affect individuals and/or their personally identifiable information;

(iv) *Individual choice.* Individuals should be provided a reasonable opportunity and capability to make informed decisions about the collection, use, and disclosure of their personally identifiable information;

(v) *Collection, use, and disclosure limitations.* Personally identifiable information should be created, collected, used, and/or disclosed only to the extent necessary to accomplish a specified purpose(s) and never to discriminate inappropriately;

(vi) *Data quality and integrity.* Persons and entities should take reasonable steps to ensure that personally identifiable information is complete, accurate, and up-to-date to the extent necessary for the person's or entity's intended purposes and has not been altered or destroyed in an unauthorized manner;

(vii) *Safeguards.* Personally identifiable information should be protected with reasonable operational, administrative, technical, and physical safeguards to ensure its confidentiality, integrity, and availability and to prevent unauthorized or inappropriate access, use, or disclosure; and,

(viii) *Accountability.* These principles should be implemented, and adherence assured, through appropriate monitoring and other means and methods should be in place to report and mitigate non-adherence and breaches.

(4) For the purposes of implementing the principle described in paragraph (a)(3)(vii) of this section, the Exchange must establish and implement operational, technical, administrative and physical safeguards that are consistent with any applicable laws (including this section) to ensure—

(i) The confidentiality, integrity, and availability of personally identifiable information created, collected, used, and/or disclosed by the Exchange;

(ii) Personally identifiable information is only used by or disclosed to those authorized to receive or view it;

(iii) Return information, as such term is defined by section 6103(b)(2) of the Code, is kept confidential under section 6103 of the Code;

(iv) Personally identifiable information is protected against any reasonably anticipated threats or hazards to the confidentiality, integrity, and availability of such information;

(v) Personally identifiable information is protected against any reasonably anticipated uses or disclosures of such information that are not permitted or required by law; and

(vi) Personally identifiable information is securely destroyed or disposed of in an appropriate and reasonable manner and in accordance with retention schedules;

(5) The Exchange must monitor, periodically assess, and update the security controls and related system risks to ensure the continued effectiveness of those controls.

(6) The Exchange must develop and utilize secure electronic interfaces when sharing personally identifiable information electronically.

(b) *Application to non-Exchange entities.* Except for tax return information, which is governed by section 6103 of the Code, when collection, use or disclosure is not otherwise required by law, an Exchange must require the same or more stringent privacy and security standards (as § 155.260(a)) as a condition of contract or agreement with individuals or entities, such as Navigators, agents, and brokers, that:

(1) Gain access to personally identifiable information submitted to an Exchange; or

(2) Collect, use or disclose personally identifiable information gathered directly from applicants, qualified individuals, or enrollees while that individual or entity is performing the functions outlined in the agreement with the Exchange.

(c) *Workforce compliance.* The Exchange must ensure its workforce complies with the policies and procedures developed and implemented by the Exchange to comply with this section.

(d) *Written policies and procedures.* Policies and procedures regarding the creation collection, use, and disclosure of personally identifiable information must, at minimum:

(1) Be in writing, and available to the Secretary of HHS upon request; and

(2) Identify applicable law governing collection, use, and disclosure of personally identifiable information.

(e) *Data sharing.* Data matching and sharing arrangements that facilitate the sharing of personally identifiable information between the Exchange and agencies administering Medicaid, CHIP or the BHP for the exchange of eligibility information must:

(1) Meet any applicable requirements described in this section;

(2) Meet any applicable requirements described in section 1413(c)(1) and (c)(2) of the Affordable Care Act;

(3) Be equal to or more stringent than the requirements for Medicaid programs under section 1942 of the Act; and

(4) For those matching agreements that meet the definition of "matching program" under 5 U.S.C. 552a(a)(8), comply with 5 U.S.C. 552a(o).

(f) *Compliance with the Code.* Return information, as defined in section 6103(b)(2) of the Code, must be kept confidential and disclosed, used, and maintained only in accordance with section 6103 of the Code.

(g) *Improper use and disclosure of information.* Any person who knowingly and willfully uses or discloses information in violation of section 1411(g) of the Affordable Care Act will be subject to a civil penalty of not more than $25,000 per person or entity, per use or disclosure, in addition to other penalties that may be prescribed by law.

Author Contact Information

Suzanne M. Kirchhoff
Analyst in Health Care Financing
skirchhoff@crs.loc.gov, 7-0658

www.ingramcontent.com/pod-product-compliance
Lightning Source LLC
Chambersburg PA
CBHW080737290526
45790CB00008B/3230